Guilt

....

Escaping Its Strong Hold

Lauren Whitman

New
Growth
Press

newgrowthpress.com

New Growth Press, Greensboro, NC 27401
Copyright © 2022 by Lauren Whitman

Cover Design: Dan Stelzer
Interior Design and Typesetting: Gretchen Logterman

ISBN: 978-1-64507-265-2 (Print)
ISBN: 978-1-64507-266-9 (eBook)

Library of Congress Cataloging-in-Publication Data

Printed in India

29 28 27 26 25 24 23 22   1 2 3 4 5

The first time I struggled with mom guilt was on the very day that I became a mother.

As many pregnant mothers do, I had carefully crafted a birth plan for my daughter's hospital delivery. In the months leading up to my due date, I did hours of research. I talked to my doctor. I talked to other mothers. I wrote and refined the draft of the plan. I printed out copies of it for anyone who would need it at the hospital. I was ready. I fully expected that all would go according to plan.

But all did not go according to plan. And in my first days of motherhood, I struggled. I had failed. My birth plan represented what I had conceived of as *the best* for my baby's entrance into the world, and I had failed to give that to her. And so in the months of learning to be a mom and focusing on my newborn, I was simultaneously fixating on this failure.

The Pervasive Experience of Mom Guilt

This was my grim entrance into the experience of mom guilt. I soon discovered it could be pervasive, intruding into any situation or decision regarding my child. Mom guilt has many faces, and the burden can be heavy. Here are a few ways we can experience the weight of its condemnation:

- From our own self-evaluations: *I'm failing as a mom. I am not good enough.* It can sound like this: "I wasn't able to produce enough milk to breastfeed. My baby isn't getting what is best for him and it's my fault."

- From our struggles with motherhood: *I didn't know being a mom would feel so hard all the time. Why do I find my kids so difficult?*

- From our sense of responsibility for everything that goes wrong. This starts when our kids are young but grows along with them. We often feel responsible for our children's poor choices. This is especially true when they are young adults and their choices have bigger, more public consequences. It's easy to have a growing list of "if only I had done this . . . or that . . .".

From these examples, we see that *mom guilt* can be used to describe diverse situations and internal struggles. Here, then, is a definition for this experience:

> Mom guilt is a hyper-awareness of the "shoulds" of parenting and fixates on ways you see yourself failing. This everyday experience is persistent, and even faith in Jesus doesn't seem to quiet these feelings of inadequacy.

Mom Guilt versus True Guilt

In this definition, notice that mom guilt is different from true, biblical guilt. True guilt comes after we have sinned. Of course, there are daily instances when moms sin against their kids. For example, if I'm angry at my child's behavior, shame her, and feel guilty after I do, then my guilt is actually helpful, as it can lead me to repent before the Lord and seek my child's forgiveness for my harshness. God allows us to feel guilt so that we do something important and necessary: confess and repent to him and to those we have hurt. But the mom guilt I'm talking about is different. It is false and deceptive guilt that fills our thoughts and impacts how we feel about ourselves and our mothering. It is a form of suffering, and my goal is to locate how God helps moms escape from the strong hold of mom guilt.

Because mom guilt covers a wide range of experiences, it can be confusing to discern what gives rise to it. So first we will identify common roots of mom guilt. Doing so will help us understand what is happening when we feel it. Second, we will uncover a biblical perspective on those roots, which then helps guide our responses. Finally, I'd like for you to ask someone close to you—your husband, a trusted friend, or a relative—to read this booklet. I have included a note to that person on the last page so that you can have their help.

Common Roots of Mom Guilt

Just as tree roots provide a base of support to a tree's trunk and branches, the roots of mom guilt support its growth in our hearts. Here are four common roots of mom guilt.

Root #1: Our flawed view of our limitations

Every person is limited in what they are able to do. We are creatures and not the Creator, and therefore we cannot do all things. Furthermore, we are creatures who differ in ability from each other. An ability that comes easily to one mom might not come easily to another mom, and all of this is out of our control. We don't always interpret our own set of limitations this way, however. Sometimes moms are tempted to interpret limitations as personal failures—as if we should be capable in every way. This is an unattainable expectation! This keeps the mom who did not produce enough breast milk stuck in mom guilt. She interprets this as a personal failure of hers and berates herself about it.

Similarly, a flawed view of limitations keeps a working mom in mom guilt. When she can't make it to her teenager's soccer game because of work obligations, she feels guilty even though her job is part of what provides for the family's needs. As much as moms would love to be in two places at once, we can't be.

Root #2: False standards

There are two categories of standards when it comes to measuring our "success" as moms—those we create ourselves and those imposed upon us. Let's look at both.

First, we generate our own standards. We create an image of an ideal mom based on who we want or wish to be as a mother. Maybe your ideal mom does not permit her kids to watch television, but instead keeps them busy with reading and chores. Perhaps she always knows how to implement discipline that results in her children's prompt, sincere repentance.

Whatever your ideal mom looks like, we often create her with good intentions. It's helpful to have role models and aspire to certain characteristics for the roles that we are in. But this can become distorted if we start to view them as standards that we *should* or *must* live up to. We start to see high standards as more than aspirational and begin to see them as achievements we expect ourselves to reach. This can result in mom guilt for reasons that relate back to our human limitations. Oftentimes, our creaturely limitations bump up against this idealized version of ourselves.

At other times, our expectations for what mothering our kids "should" feel like bumps up against reality. The reality is that parenting is a challenge. It's a blessing and a privilege, of course. But it's hard—and it's normal for it to *feel* hard. And it's even common and normal when there are aspects of our kids' personalities that we find challenging, given our own personalities and preferences. To think that we would not or should not ever feel, think, or wrestle with such things is a false standard.

Second, societal and cultural standards are imposed upon us. In Western society, the ideal model of parenting is called *intensive parenting*. Research shows that across both socioeconomic and cultural lines, there is wide agreement among parents that this is the ideal way to parent. Author Sharon Hays describes intensive parenting as "child-centered, expert-guided, emotionally absorbing, labor-intensive, and financially expensive."[1] Hays notes that all societies develop norms for parenting and that it's hard not to see your society's norms as *the only correct way* to parent. I will not focus here on the strengths and weaknesses of intensive parenting; rather, I raise it so that we can gain an awareness of our sociohistorical moment, because I believe it contributes to mom guilt.

For example, if members of our society largely agree that we are to parent in a child-centered way, then it makes sense that moms struggle with guilt when we do something such as go out for an evening with our friends. Are we being selfish when we take care of ourselves or invest in ourselves, when that time might have been time spent investing in our kids? Are we limiting their potential if we don't invest in the premium options available for their schooling or extracurricular activities?

A closely related societal norm that moms face is living up to the image of "Supermom." Supermom must do it all for her kids and have it all together—all of the time. She keeps tabs on all the research related to raising competent, well-adjusted children, is up to date on the latest products that will enhance her children's development, cooks three nutritious meals from scratch every day, works patiently with the kids on homework after dinner, and gets all of them bathed and in bed on schedule each night.

Perhaps you do not resonate with some of these examples because you are from a different culture with different norms for mothering. But no matter where or when you live, it's important to be aware that society projects standards of good mothering onto mothers, and we are vulnerable to the feeling that we must live up to them.

So whether we impose false standards on ourselves or feel burdened by those of our culture, this root of mom guilt shows us that we must identify the ideals that leave us feeling that we have fallen short, don't measure up, and are not enough.

Root #3: Negatively comparing ourselves to other moms

Sometimes we feel mom guilt when other moms excel in ways that we don't. The use of social media makes us especially vulnerable to comparison because we see images and read stories about what other moms do with their kids. Imagine if a mom sees adorable pictures on Instagram of another mom doing crafts with her cooperative and engaged children. If you're the mom who isn't good at crafts or whose kids can't sit still for this kind of activity, then you can easily feel mom guilt because you do not provide your kids with this experience.

Root #4: Fear

Fear is present in all of these roots because we deeply care about our kids. We want them to grow up well, and anything that seems to threaten that hope makes us feel afraid. But sometimes feelings that we recognize can mask deeper feelings that are harder to identify. In this case, we may respond to a difficulty in our kids' lives with mom guilt, not recognizing the fear and helplessness that lie beneath it. Fear morphs into guilt as we turn on *ourselves* as a way to control what we don't have control over. As I fixate on my role in the situation, I feel guilt because

I'm identifying what I could have done or should have done. Mom guilt feels miserable, but sometimes it is less scary than facing our powerlessness against all the things that seem to threaten our children's well-being.

This is the dynamic at play for Leah, a mom whose adult children are making unwise life choices. Fear is at the root of her mom guilt. Her kids aren't living in ways that reflect the values that she and her husband raised them to have. She is afraid of what this means about their futures. She is afraid of what it means about where they stand with the Lord. She is afraid of what others think of her kids. But those fears are buried under mom guilt and she focuses on herself, trying to identify where she failed. What could she have done differently that would have steered them in a different direction? How is she to blame for how they've turned out? Her fear-driven thoughts and emotions create an unhelpful focus on herself and the past.

These four roots can result in mom guilt that has a strong hold on our thoughts and emotions. Are there other roots that come to mind for you? An awareness of them can help you identify and parse out what is going on in the midst of these experiences. Sometimes one root will be predominant in giving rise to mom guilt. Sometimes it will be more than one; roots are usually tangled up together.

And so I want to offer a way forward for when you are struggling. You start by noticing when you feel mom guilt, and then you dig deeper to discern what is at the root of the feeling. Once you have a clearer sense of why you are struggling, you can consider how to respond.

Digging Up the Roots of Mom Guilt

How can we dig up and destroy the roots so that we can escape the strong hold of mom guilt? We will revisit each root to see how God's Word guides us, and how his ways help us.

Root #1: Our flawed view of our limitations

To be human means we are fundamentally limited. God has deemed it good and right to give people constraints of time, energy, and natural ability. He alone is limitless, and he means for our limitations to lead us to a place of rightful dependence on him. God does not disdain us for our lack in any of these areas. Psalm 103 says that he feels compassion for us as he sees us in our weaknesses. There is something about us being weak—being dust, as Psalm 103:14 says—that stirs up his heart for us. In contrast, mom guilt offers no grace and gentleness, no recognition of human weakness.

We also face limitations because we live in a world of sin and suffering, in which things don't always work as they should. Think again of the mom who can't breastfeed. There is a place for this mom to feel sad and feel the loss of this ability. Were the world not broken, she would not suffer from this inability. So it will help her to acknowledge the loss and feel the sadness. Sometimes we will need to lead ourselves to the appropriate emotional responses, given the realities of our situation. In her case, sadness and grief are appropriate; mom guilt is not. Feeling disappointment helped me, too, after my daughter's birth. My body didn't go through labor the way I had hoped it would—but that didn't mean there was guilt I had to bear as if I had done something wrong. I had to learn to reject the guilt and work through my sadness.

There are other times that we will discern personal limitations that we can work on and grow in. Here's an example: Yu-Jun struggles with creating structure and keeping rhythms in day-to-day life. She has never had a knack for organization, but before she was a mom it wasn't a problem. Now, disorganization and a sporadic schedule have obvious negative consequences. Her mom guilt thoughts sound like self-disgust: *I'm like a tornado. I can't keep track of anything. My kids are going to hate me once they realize what chaos they are living in.* But a constructive response recognizes that creating structure is a skill that can be developed. God means for his people to be interdependent, so perhaps she seeks help from a friend who does have a knack for organization. Instead of giving in to the condemnation of mom guilt, she can instead commit to grow so that she can give more of this good thing to her kids.

Note, however, that growth is different from perfection. Even our best efforts are imperfect and will differ from family to family.

Root #2: False standards

False standards grow strong and resilient roots. To dig them up, we start with identifying the false standards we are living under. To do this, we need to practice discernment. Is a feeling of mom guilt related to a failure to meet:

- my self-imposed standard?
- my culture's standard?
- my husband's standard?
- my friend's standard?
- my church's standard?

What's your false measuring stick?

Also consider: What does your idealized mom look like? Why do you identify these particular ideal attributes? Where do they come from, and what do they mean to you? Wrestling through these questions prepares you to loosen the grip of holding yourself to idealized standards. From there, questions like these go in a good direction: What does God call me to? Does God call me to be the mom that I have imagined, or to something else?

As we do this, we start to realize that our measuring stick is not from God. He calls mothers to faithfulness, not to an idealized version of ourselves that we (or our culture) created. We want to be more concerned with God's measure than anyone else's. What does he value? Psalm 147:10–11 is helpful here:

His pleasure is not in the strength of the horse,
    nor his delight in the legs of the warrior;
the Lord delights in those who fear him,
    who put their hope in his unfailing love.

God doesn't look for the strongest, most successful, or most capable people. That is not what pleases him.

His delight is when we fear him. He takes pleasure when we put our hope in his unfailing love.

Knowing this reorients us. Instead of:

Am I being a mom that I feel at peace with and happy with because I'm measuring up to my ideals?

our focus is more like:

As I mother today, am I placing my hope in the Lord's unfailing love, instead of hoping that I'll be a strong, capable, idealized version of myself?

The first question is radically different from the second question—and takes us to radically different places. If I'm hoping in his unfailing love instead of my own capabilities, then instead of dwelling in mom guilt perhaps I'll pray like this in a moment of struggle:

"Father, I am so tempted when I see my weaknesses to obsess about my shortcomings. I feel like a failure because of what I can't give my kids. But your love never fails. You love me, you love my kids, and so I can hope that even with my weaknesses and limitations, that you will provide what we all need."

Faithful living—not perfection. As we abandon this idealized version of ourselves, we must also pursue the matter of discovering what faithfulness in our mothering looks like. It's good to know how God made us and what gifts and skills he gave us. God calls us to steward these faithfully, which is a different and more fruitful pursuit than trying to live up to an image of a perfect mom. Self-understanding also gives us clarity on where to pursue outside help for our kids' development. We can't be all things to them. God intends for his people to live in community, and it is appropriate to look to others to help us as we raise and disciple our children. God made us different from each other on purpose (Romans 12:4–5)! It's not all on us as mothers—nor should it be. That is too heavy of a burden to bear, and God does not call us to bear it. Instead, hold tight to this: you are you, uniquely made in God's image, with a certain set of gifts and skills. With God's help, strive to be faithful to use those gifts for the blessing and benefit of your children.

There's more to see! Another way to dig up the root of unreachable standards is to make it a practice to see more than your failures. It is second nature to judge ourselves harshly and to grade ourselves on a pass/fail system, which always results in a failing mark.

Though we see failures so instinctively, here is the good news: *there is more to see.* There are places you've done well! Practice identifying where you were faithful. Doing so reflects a deeper truth: God sees you completely. God sees more than just your failures. He sees your weaknesses *and* your strengths, your failures *and* your successes. To gain this wide-angle gaze, ask yourself: Where was I faithful? What did I do well today with my kids? How did I trust the Lord with how the day unfolded?[2]

God sees more than failure in you—and he wants you to see it too so you can be encouraged.

It's good and right to take care of yourself. Another way to push back against the standards of intensive parenting is to take better care of yourself! This is a radical statement for moms who suffer from mom guilt. Yet living in a society that places intense expectations on parents is all the more reason to do this. Get the haircut you've been putting off. Schedule a walk with your friend. And do so in thankfulness, knowing that God sees the many efforts and sacrifices that you make as a mom—and that he sees you not only as a mom but also as a person who needs care and support as well.

What is achievable and sustainable? Since we live in a culture where parents often face unachievable and unsustainable expectations, it's important to prayerfully seek the Lord and ponder: What *is* achievable and sustainable for my family? What are our priorities? What are the hopes, dreams, and goals for our family, given the particular sets of skills, gifts, and abilities God has given us? How can we use those to be a blessing to one another and to the community God has us in?

Pursuing the Lord with questions like these leads to clarity and purpose. It leads away from the "shoulds" of society's parenting ideals to being centered on the greatest hope we have as Christian mothers: that our children will be disciples of Christ. When we pursue our culture's standards for parenting, we lose sight of this foundational responsibility of parenting and feel mom guilt over things that are not essential. But as we hold on to this priority, it helps us overlook, for example, the alleged "Supermom sin" of serving frozen pizza two nights in a row. If we are freed from living up to Supermom standards, then we can simply be grateful that we don't have to cook! When we keep the main thing the main thing, it helps us be lighthearted about the times we fail to meet idealized goals.

Root #3: Negatively comparing ourselves to other moms

To dig up the root of comparison, we grow in a kingdom mindset. After Jesus ascended and sent his Spirit, the kingdom of God was established on earth. His people are meant to live in ways that reflect this reality. Think of the qualities described in the Sermon on the Mount (Matthew 5–7) and the fruit of the Spirit (Galatians 5:22–23). These are kingdom-minded priorities.

When we process and respond out of a mindset that mirrors kingdom priorities, then we are concerned with questions such as, "How can I rejoice when I see other moms doing great things with their kids?" A kingdom mindset also seeks to bless your sister, so perhaps you pray a quick prayer of blessing for her—"Lord, establish the work of her hands" (see Psalm 90:17). The vision is for this to be an occasion to be glad and give glory to God, instead of making it about us and constructing a new measure for ourselves of what a good mother is supposed to look like.

We will be helped in this as we focus on God's specific call on our lives. Knowing God's call requires an accurate self-understanding of your unique set of circumstances, skills, and gifts. You can't be like other moms because you don't have the same set of circumstances, skills, or gifts. It is more fruitful to focus on how you can be faithful with the tools in your toolbox.

Let's apply this principle to the earlier example of the pictures we see on social media. Instead of mom guilt that you're not like that mom who does crafts, you can work on being glad for her family. It's wonderful that they enjoy that activity, but craft time is not prescriptive for all families! Or, if craft time seems like a worthy pursuit for your kids despite your lack of interest in it, then you can draw from her ideas, rather than seeing them as commentary on your performance. Let her ideas motivate you to invest in this activity, but for the right reasons—to bless your kids. It's great to be motivated and spurred on to good works by what we see other moms doing. But don't try to be like that mom simply because you're feeling guilty and you want to erase your mom guilt.

Let's next discuss the flip side of comparison. On one hand, we compare ourselves and we deem ourselves as failures. But we can also compare ourselves in a way that we see ourselves favorably. We criticize other moms when an aspect of their motherhood seems wrong to us. Prideful judgment is an anti-kingdom mindset and keeps the problem of mom guilt in place.

Here's an example: Candace, a stay-at-home mom, sends her toddlers to day care. You question this. Why are they in day care if she doesn't work? For you, her choice doesn't jibe with what a mother should be doing.

But humility, instead of uncharitable judgment, says, *I don't know why she made that choice*. And in this place of not knowing, God calls you to compassion and understanding, which is to believe the best of this mom because *you don't know*.

So we repent of prideful judgment of other moms. Let's build each other up by showing compassion and understanding for the choices we make as moms—and that starts in our hearts and thoughts about other moms. The vision here is to have a culture of openness—as opposed to hiding our choices from other moms because we fear their judgment. We aim for openness that leads to support and encouragement. Your friends need that. You need that.

To grow in encouraging other moms, which is another outworking of a kingdom mindset, be on the lookout for what is good and praiseworthy in their mothering. Let's grow in putting words to what we see in other moms in order to build them up and bless them (Ephesians 4:25)! Just as God sees more than your failure, how can you represent him by pointing out what is admirable in the mothers you know? Giving and receiving encouragement is one sure escape from the stronghold of mom guilt.

Root #4: Fear

To dig out fear, we must learn to pivot away from it: When I am afraid, I trust in the Lord (Psalm 56:3). If I'm afraid for my children, this is the time to trust. I turn toward the Lord. I *don't* commandeer a false sense of control through obsessing over my role in a problem. I accept my limitations. A mother isn't called to be God, and so I turn *to* God in faith. I refrain from taking on responsibility where I have none.

This reorientation trusts God with outcomes in your child's life. Moms can have a lot of impact and influence, but we don't have control over all aspects of our children's lives, including outcomes, and so we learn the act of entrusting these to God.

Remember Leah, the mom of straying young adults? To escape her mom guilt, she must learn both to identify her fears and to entrust her children to the Lord. Obsessing over how she might have failed them is torturous, and there is never any resolution to her questions because there are no simple answers as to why her kids have strayed. Instead, how can she bring her fears about her children to God? How can she entrust her children, day after day, to the Lord (Psalm 62:8)? And how might that impact how she pursues and prays for them? In contrast to mom guilt that spirals unproductively, these are fruitful pursuits.

Seeing that there are faithful responses to the roots of mom guilt, I pray that your hope is rising. There are escapes—and with God's help, I trust that you will find them.

Mom, You Are a Child of God

As we have discussed ways to escape from mom guilt, let me close by highlighting that the Lord himself initiates our escape from mom guilt. He rescues us from this powerful enemy that is too strong for us (Psalm 18:17). He fights for you. He rescues you because he delights in you (Psalm 18:19). Knowing that God is like this, we have every good reason to believe that he helps us with mom guilt. Isn't this what any good father would do for his child? He *is* a good Father—and you are his child. To be a mother is a great and high calling—but you, mom, are first and foremost your Father's beloved child (John 1:12; 2 Corinthians 6:18). Cling to that when you are struggling with mom guilt—and then join your Father in his fight.

Here is a summary of how to do that. First, *remember* that you are God's child—a child who needs her Father's help, because these feelings are hard, painful, and threaten to steal the joy of being a mother from you. Now *run* to your Father because he is the One who rescues you. And from that place of knowing you are a child who is not on her own but is under the care of her kind Father, dig deeper to *discern* what root or roots give rise to mom guilt this time. From there, *respond* to the particulars of what is taking hold of your heart. Respond so that mom guilt is ousted, because it has no rightful place in your life. Mom guilt is an intruder, and it doesn't belong.

Remember. Run. Discern the roots. Respond in faith. And trust that God is compassionate toward you and is with you to help when you experience mom guilt.

A Note to Husbands and Others Who Support Moms

Hello! By reading this book, I hope you have grown in your understanding of what the experience of mom guilt is like. It is a formidable foe your wife or loved one faces, and your help will bless her tremendously. With that in mind, here are four ideas for how you can partner with her in this battle.

1. I asked moms to make it a practice to see beyond their perceived failures and identify what they have done well. This is a place where you can bless her because you have the privilege to see her up close in day-to-day life. You can represent the God who sees, and who sees us with eyes of compassion and tenderness, by regularly naming the ways you see her serving, doing well, and being faithful with her children. For a husband, this can be a simple observation such as, "I appreciate how you responded to our son when he talked back to you. You were firm and clear as to why that was wrong." Be intentional to put words to what you see in her, with the goal that she is encouraged. Do this daily.

2. Ask your wife or loved one about her particular experience of mom guilt. Ask her, "What is this like for you?" As fair warning, so you don't think you did something wrong, know that she might respond with tears, which is actually a good thing. It means she trusts you, and it will

help her to cry freely about things that weigh her down. Invite her to put her mom guilt into words—and then speak into those thoughts. You can help her see clearly by reflecting the Father's heart toward her, which might sound like this: "It makes me sad when you blame yourself for things that clearly aren't your fault." Reassure her in those areas she thinks she is failing as a mom. Your voice matters. You can interrupt the steady stream of mom guilt thoughts. Pray with her, specifically, for the help she needs.

3. If there is a challenge in her child's life, she might feel that she is responsible for the outcomes. She might be concerned that she has contributed to, or even caused, the problem through her perceived failures. Remind her, "This isn't all on you." Pray together about the issues with the child. Be with her in it all.

4. Remind her that perfection isn't the goal. Being Supermom isn't the goal. Faithfulness to God is the goal. And for the times we blow it, we will find him eager to show us his grace and mercy.

Thank you for your help.

Gratefully,
Lauren

Endnotes

1. Sharon Hays, *The Cultural Contradictions of Motherhood* (New Haven, CT: Yale University Press, 1998), 8.

2. For more on the theme of God seeing more than failure in our mothering, see Lauren Whitman, "Mom Guilt and the God Who Sees," CCEF, August 19, 2021, https://www.ccef.org/mom-guilt-and-the-god-who-sees.